NO LONGER PROPERTY OF
KING COUNTY LIBRARY SYSTEM

NOV   2011

A Guide to
AMERICAN STATES

New Hampshire

THE GRANITE STATE

www.av2books.com

AV² provides enriched content that supplements and complements this book. Weigl's AV² books strive to create inspired learning and engage young minds in a total learning experience.

Your AV² Media Enhanced books come alive with...

Audio
Listen to sections of the book read aloud.

Key Words
Study vocabulary, and complete a matching word activity.

Go to **www.av2books.com**, and enter this book's unique code.

Video
Watch informative video clips.

Quizzes
Test your knowledge.

BOOK CODE

E 9 2 5 5 4 4

Embedded Weblinks
Gain additional information for research.

Slide Show
View images and captions, and prepare a presentation.

AV² by Weigl brings you media enhanced books that support active learning.

Try This!
Complete activities and hands-on experiments.

... and much, much more!

Published by AV² by Weigl
350 5th Avenue, 59th Floor
New York, NY 10118
Website: www.av2books.com   www.weigl.com

Copyright 2012 AV² by Weigl
All rights reserved. No part of this publication may be reproduced, stored in a retrieval system, or transmitted in any form or by any means, electronic, mechanical, photocopying, recording, or otherwise, without the prior written permission of the publisher.

Library of Congress Cataloging-in-Publication Data

Craats, Rennay.
 New Hampshire / Rennay Craats.
    p. cm. -- (A guide to American states)
 Includes index.
 ISBN 978-1-61690-801-0 (hardcover : alk. paper) -- ISBN 978-1-61690-477-7 (online)
 1. New Hampshire--Juvenile literature. I. Title.
 F34.3.C733 2011
 974.2--dc23
                    2011018521

Printed in the United States of America in North Mankato, Minnesota

052011
WEP180511

Project Coordinator Jordan McGill
Art Director Terry Paulhus

Photo Credits
Every reasonable effort has been made to trace ownership and to obtain permission to reprint copyright material. The publishers would be pleased to have any errors or omissions brought to their attention so that they may be corrected in subsequent printings.

Weigl acknowledges Getty Images as its primary image supplier for this title.

Contents

Dartmouth College in Hanover was founded in 1769. John Wentworth, the royal governor of New Hampshire, provided the land on which it was built.

Introduction

New Hampshire is one of the original 13 colonies. On January 5, 1776, New Hampshire adopted its own **constitution** and became the first state to proclaim itself independent from Great Britain. New Hampshire's announcement came six months before the Declaration of Independence.

New Hampshire played a major role in the American Revolution. As early as December 1774 rebels began fighting against British rule. The rebels forced the British-appointed governor, John Wentworth, out of the colony and a new **revolutionary** government took over. While no battles took place in the state during the American Revolution, it was important to the cause.

White Mountain National Forest contains some of the highest elevations in New England, including Mount Washington.

Colonel John Stark and his regiment from New Hampshire fought at the Battle of Bunker Hill in 1775. It was an important colonial victory in the first months of the American Revolution.

Portsmouth became a key town in the war. From there, privately owned vessels, or privateers, were launched to attack British ships. New Hampshire soldiers also came to the aid of Massachusetts rebels once the battles of Lexington and Concord erupted in 1775.

New Hampshire supplied several strong military leaders to the **Continental Army**, including John Stark and John Sullivan. Stark fought at the battles of Bunker Hill, Trenton, and Princeton. In August 1777, Stark and his men helped turn the tide of the war when they prevented the British forces from stealing much-needed supplies at Bennington. Then, in 1779, John Sullivan defeated a powerful British force and its Iroquois supporters at Newtown, New York.

Since 1920 the long road to the White House has begun in New Hampshire. Every four years the state holds the first **presidential primary election**. New Hampshire has one of the country's highest voter turnouts.

Where Is New Hampshire?

New Hampshire is located in the northeastern United States. Getting to New Hampshire is as easy as boarding a plane or climbing into a car. More than 17,000 miles of highway carry traffic into and out of the state. For air travelers, Manchester Airport, the state's largest airport, is a major destination. In addition, there are more than 20 other airports in the state. While New Hampshire's miles of railroad track are used less today than in the past, some trains still offer sightseeing trips. These trips provide visitors with a memorable way to experience the state.

New Hampshire Motor Speedway in Loudon hosts professional auto races. It also runs a training school that teaches teenagers to drive safer and smarter on the state's many roads and highways.

About 10,000 years ago all of New Hampshire was buried beneath **glaciers**. These glaciers created the amazing landscape found in the state. The glaciers chiseled and molded the mountains. As these ice masses melted, they created countless lakes, streams, and rivers. One of the state's nicknames is the Mother of Rivers.

New Hampshire's other nicknames also refer to the distinct landscapes found in the state. Plentiful granite deposits earned New Hampshire its most popular nickname as the Granite State. The nickname White Mountain State draws attention to the grand and rugged mountain range in the northern part of the state. Lastly, New Hampshire is often referred to as the Switzerland of America because of the stunning mountain scenery, matched only by the Alps.

I DIDN'T KNOW THAT!

The New Hampshire Turnpike was completed in 1950.

New Hampshire has 10 counties, 13 municipalities, and 221 towns.

New Hampshire covers almost 9,000 square miles.

New Hampshire's 13-mile coastline on the Atlantic Ocean is the shortest of any state that borders an ocean.

One nickname for New Hampshire, Mother of Rivers, recognizes that five large New England rivers start in the granite hills of New Hampshire. It is also a reflection of the hundreds of lakes, ponds, and rivers found throughout the state.

Mapping New Hampshire

New Hampshire is one of six New England states. The others are Connecticut, Maine, Massachusetts, Rhode Island, and Vermont. To the east of New Hampshire lie Maine and the waters of the Atlantic Ocean. Massachusetts forms New Hampshire's southern border, and Vermont makes up its western edge. The state shares its northern border with the Canadian province of Quebec.

Sites and Symbols

STATE SEAL
New Hampshire

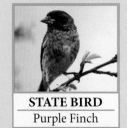

STATE BIRD
Purple Finch

STATE FLOWER
Purple Lilac

STATE FLAG
New Hampshire

STATE ANIMAL
White-tailed Deer

STATE TREE
White Birch

Nickname The Granite State

Motto Live Free or Die

Song "Old New Hampshire," words by John F. Holmes and music by Maurice Hoffmann

Entered the Union June 21, 1788, as the 9th state

Capital Concord

Population (2010 Census) 1,316,470 Ranked 42nd state

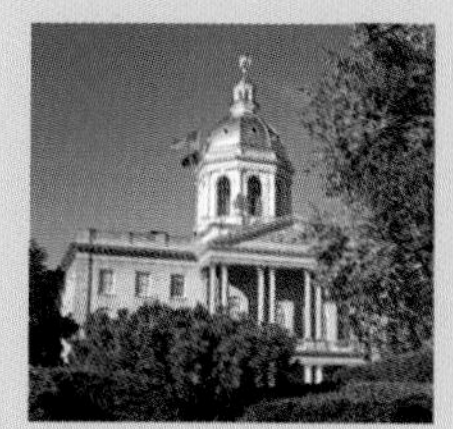

STATE CAPITAL

Concord, settled in 1727, lies along the Merrimack River. Massachusetts incorporated the village as Rumford in 1733. It was renamed Concord by New Hampshire in 1765 and became New Hampshire's capital city in 1808. More than 42,000 people live in Concord.

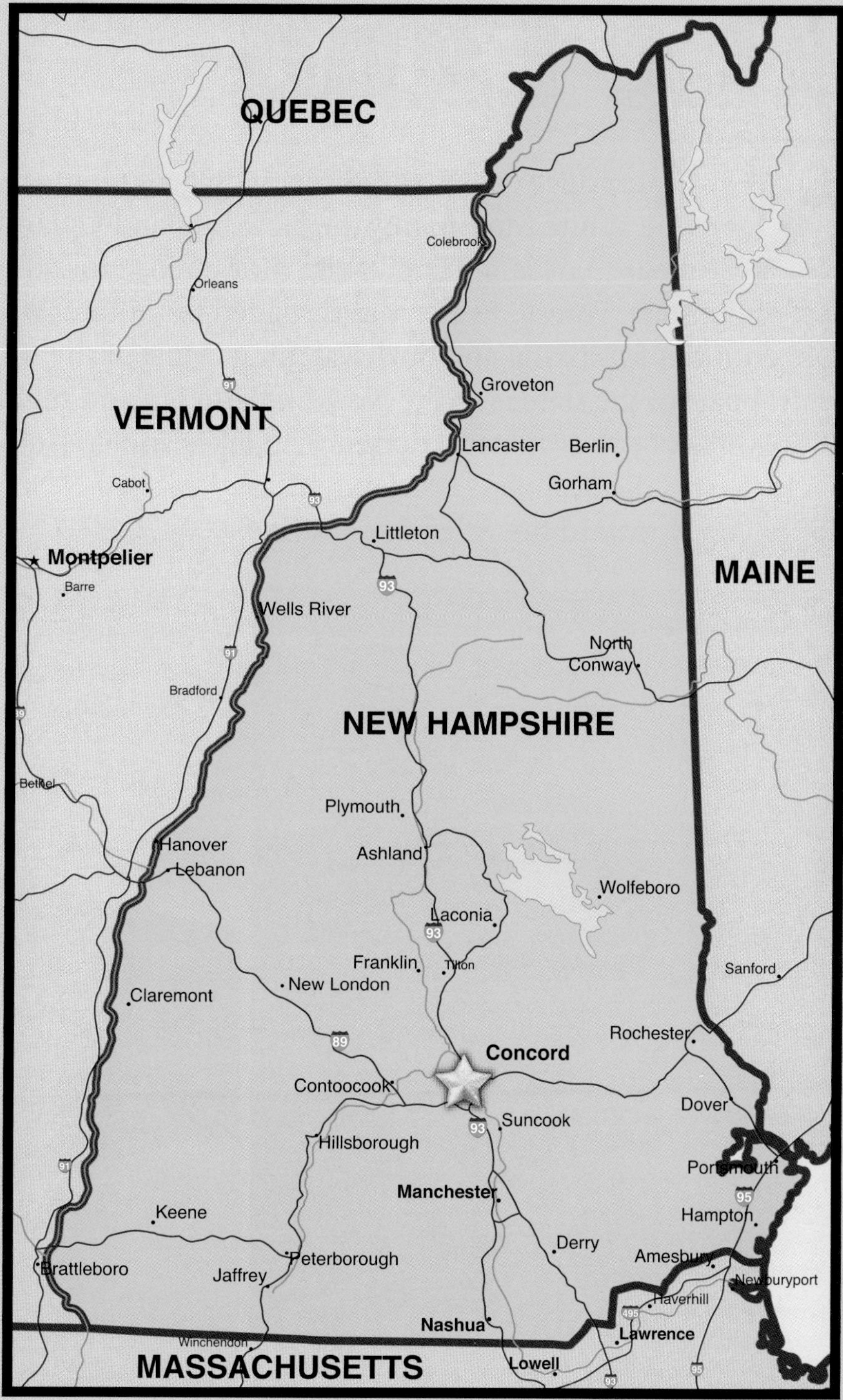

QUEBEC
VERMONT
NEW HAMPSHIRE
MAINE
MASSACHUSETTS
Colebrook
Orleans
Groveton
Lancaster
Berlin
Gorham
Cabot
Littleton
Montpelier
Barre
Wells River
North Conway
Bradford
Bethel
Plymouth
Ashland
Hanover
Lebanon
Wolfeboro
Laconia
Franklin
Tilton
New London
Claremont
Sanford
Rochester
Concord
Contoocook
Suncook
Dover
Hillsborough
Portsmouth
Manchester
Hampton
Keene
Derry
Amesbury
Peterborough
Brattleboro
Jaffrey
Newburyport
Haverhill
Nashua
Lawrence
Winchendon
Lowell
93
91
89
95
495

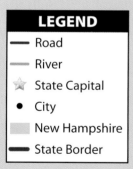

LEGEND

- Road
- River
- State Capital
- City
- New Hampshire
- State Border

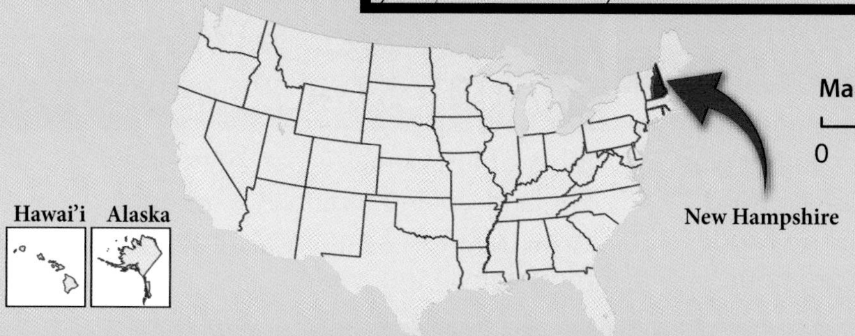

Hawai'i
Alaska
New Hampshire

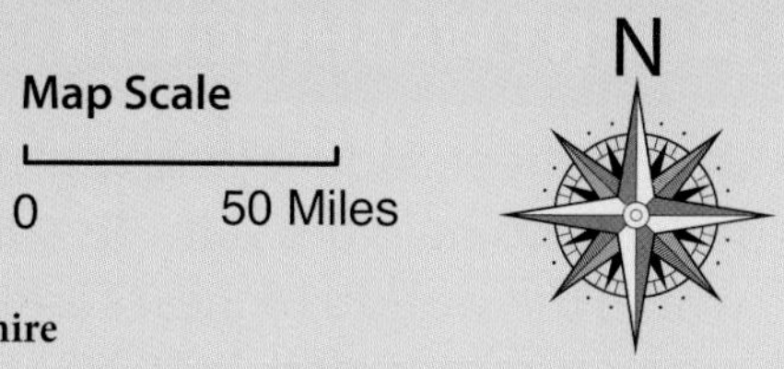

Map Scale
0
50 Miles
N

The Land

New Hampshire consists of three main geographic regions. They are the White Mountains, the New England Upland, and the Seaboard Lowland. The White Mountains cross the northern part of the state. Forested valleys and rugged mountains provide ample opportunities for hiking and bird-watching. Most of the southern and central part of the state is in the New England Upland region. The rolling hills of this region are dotted with lakes and crisscrossed by rivers. Lastly, the Seaboard Lowland, in southeastern New Hampshire, slopes gently toward the Atlantic coastline.

MOUNT WASHINGTON

At 6,288 feet, Mount Washington is the highest point in the state. Its summit was where the world's highest surface wind speed was recorded, in 1934. The wind blew at a speed of 231 miles per hour.

MOUNT MONADNOCK

Mount Monadnock is part of the New England Upland region. It is thought to be the most frequently climbed mountain in the world.

CONNECTICUT RIVER

New Hampshire has approximately 40 rivers. The state's longest river is the Connecticut River, which forms the western border with Vermont. In some places, covered bridges span the river to connect the two states.

SEABOARD LOWLAND

The Seaboard Lowland is where New Hampshire borders the Atlantic Ocean. Odiorne Point State Park in Rye is part of this geographic area.

The Old Man of the Mountain above Echo Lake was a well-known landmark. The 40-foot rock formation was a natural phenomenon created 2,000 years ago by slowly moving glaciers. It collapsed in 2003, though photographs of the Old Man of the Mountain remain.

Water is an important New Hampshire feature. The state has more than 1,300 lakes and ponds.

New Hampshire operates more than 75 state park locations, including Franconia Notch State Park, Daniel Webster Birthplace State Historic Site, and North Hampton State Beach.

The Mount Washington Observatory operates a mountaintop weather station. The observatory works to improve understanding of Earth's weather and climate.

Climate

I n July, average temperatures range from 65° Fahrenheit in the north to 70° F in the south. New Hampshire's highest recorded temperature was 106° F in Nashua on July 4, 1911. In January, the average temperature is 12° F in the north and 22° F in the south. The lowest temperature ever recorded in the state was –47° F on Mount Washington on January 29, 1934. People who live in New Hampshire are expert shovelers, as heavy snowfalls are common during winter.

Average Annual Precipitation Across New Hampshire

Precipitation varies across New Hampshire. What factors might explain why Mount Washington gets so much more rainfall than places such as Lebanon? Why might Nashua and Rochester get similar amounts of precipitation?

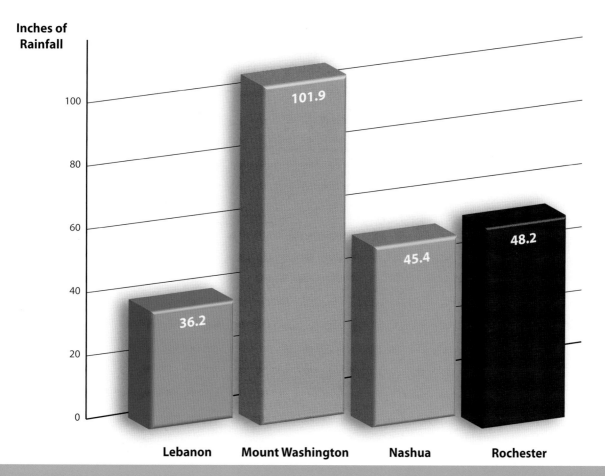

Natural Resources

With a nickname of the Granite State, it makes sense that granite is a top natural resource in New Hampshire. Granite, which is a very hard, gray stone, is one of the most important and valuable minerals in New Hampshire. The state has granite **quarries**. Some of the granite mined in New Hampshire is used in construction. Other valuable minerals in the state are sand and gravel. These are found throughout New Hampshire and make up more than half of the state's mineral output.

Granite quarries in New England have provided the stone for many important American buildings. New Hampshire granite was used in the original Smithsonian Institution in Washington, D.C.

Another natural resource that gives the state economy a boost is forestland. Timber is used largely in the pulp and paper industry. It is also used to build such products as **railroad ties**, cabinets, and furniture.

Forestland covers more than 80 percent of New Hampshire.

I DIDN'T KNOW THAT!

Large deposits of sand and gravel were left behind by melting glaciers in what is now New Hampshire.

The earth symbols of New Hampshire celebrate the state's unique geology. The official mineral is **beryl**, the official rock is granite, and the official gem is smoky quartz. Smoky quartz is found in many types of rocks, including granite.

During the colonial period, stagecoaches and the masts on warships were built using New Hampshire timber.

Forestry contributes more than $1 billion to New Hampshire's economy each year. To help preserve New Hampshire's forests, the state government taxes timber only after it has been cut.

Plants

New Hampshire is one of the most forested states in the country. More than four-fifths of New Hampshire's land is covered in trees. Evergreen forests of spruce and fir trees blanket the north, and white pine, maple, and oak trees cover parts of southern and central New Hampshire. The state's official tree is the white birch.

Hundreds of different wildflowers cover the forest floors, including wild asters, black-eyed Susans, daisies, and buttercups. The state's official flower, the purple lilac, is relatively new to New Hampshire. It was brought from Britain and planted at Governor Wentworth's home in 1750. It was chosen as the state flower because it is hardy and strong, like the people who live in New Hampshire.

NORTHERN RED OAK TREE

Many kinds of oak trees grow in New Hampshire. The northern red oak is a fast-growing tree that can reach 90 feet. It is one of the best oak for lumber.

WHITE BIRCH TREE

White birch trees, which typically grow to be 60 feet tall, are also known as canoe or paper birches. The bark of the tree peels in thin layers and was once used as writing paper and for making canoes.

ASTERS

Asters provide bees and other insects with nectar and pollen as they prepare for winter. These common wildflowers bloom in late summer.

PINK LADY SLIPPERS

The pink lady slipper is the official wildflower of the state. This flower is native to New Hampshire and grows well in the moist, wooded areas of the state.

It is not easy to tap maple trees for syrup. It takes about 40 gallons of sap to make about 1 gallon of maple syrup. Cold nights and warm days are needed for the sap to "run."

Many different shrubs take root beneath the state's trees. The American yew, red osier, hobblebush, and flowering mountain laurel shrubs are all common throughout New Hampshire.

Animals

A variety of animals roam New Hampshire's wilderness areas. Of the large animals in the state, the white-tailed deer is the most common. Snowshoe hares, mice, shrews, and squirrels all call the state home. Other animals common to New Hampshire include beavers, bears, moose, porcupines, minks, foxes, and bobcats.

People in New Hampshire have plenty of bird-watching opportunities. Black-capped chickadees, woodpeckers, and white-throated sparrows can all be found in the state. The declining populations of other birds, including the loon, the northern harrier, and the woodcock, have concerned conservationists.

New Hampshire's waterways are brimming with fish. Lake trout and landlocked salmon swim the state's deep lakes. Bass, pickerel, and perch make their homes in the state's shallow lakes and ponds.

WHITE-TAILED DEER

White-tailed deer weigh between 100 and 300 pounds. They are excellent runners, capable of traveling up to 30 miles an hour.

SPOTTED NEWT

The spotted newt is the official state amphibian. The skin of young spotted newts is toxic, and their bright red color serves as a warning to possible attackers to stay away.

BOBCAT

Bobcats are named for their short tail, which resembles a bob or a knob. Bobcats are most active at night and usually live and hunt alone.

KARNER BLUE BUTTERFLY

The Karner blue butterfly has a wingspan of about one inch. These small butterflies are **endangered** because their food source, wild lupine, has declined. Lupine grows in clearings after wildfires, and the successful prevention of these fires has reduced the lupine in the area.

I DIDN'T KNOW THAT!

The ladybug is the official insect of New Hampshire. These insects are considered to be good luck.

New Hampshire has several official state animals. The state freshwater fish is the brook trout, the state dog is the Chinook sled dog, and the state bird is the purple finch.

The peregrine falcon is an endangered species. This bird of prey is protected in the Lake Umbagog National Wildlife Refuge.

Tourism

Every summer more than 1 million people visit New Hampshire to enjoy its picturesque beauty and outdoor activities. One tourist destination is filled with mystery. Known as America's Stonehenge, this ancient structure combines astronomy with stone masonry. While no one knows for certain how the stone maze got there or which civilization built it, many archaeologists believe that it may have been a prehistoric calendar used by American Indians. The structure can still be used to determine solar and lunar events during the year. Historic artifacts found at America's Stonehenge, such as pottery, tools, and scripts, have fascinated archaeologists and visitors to New Hampshire for decades.

WHITE MOUNTAIN NATIONAL FOREST

White Mountain National Forest covers about 800,000 acres of land and offers many hiking trails. It registers more visitors each year than Yellowstone and Yosemite national parks combined.

CANNON MOUNTAIN

A state-owned ski area, Cannon Mountain is located in beautiful Franconia Notch State Park. Cannon Mountain was the site of North America's first aerial passenger tramway, built in 1938. In 1980, a renovated tramway, traveling at a speed of 1,500 feet per minute, carried its first passengers.

LAKE WINNIPESAUKEE

New Hampshire's lakes are some of the most beautiful in New England. The state's largest lake, Lake Winnipesaukee, draws swimmers, sunbathers, and kayakers from near and far.

MOUNT WASHINGTON COG RAILWAY

Many visitors travel to Bretton Woods to ride the world's first mountain-climbing cog railway. The Mount Washington Cog Railway, built in 1869, pulls the train up a steep hill using toothed cog gears and rack rails.

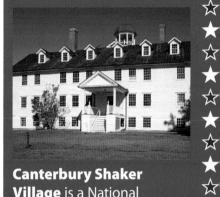

Canterbury Shaker Village is a National Historic Landmark and museum where visitors can see 25 restored original Shaker buildings.

The town of Newbury established a creative tourism center in 1999. It is housed in the **caboose** of an old train.

The American Independence Museum, in Exeter, provides an interactive look at colonial life during the American Revolution. Among its permanent collections are early American furniture, ceramics, and an original published copy of the Declaration of Independence from 1776.

Industry

Trees are the source of a valuable industry in New Hampshire. For six weeks every year hundreds of farmers tap maple trees for sap to make maple sugar, sugar candies, and maple syrup. Factors such as the health and age of the trees and the right weather affect a farm's maple syrup production. In a good year, this industry contributes about $4 million to the state's economy.

Industries in New Hampshire
Value of Goods and Services in Millions of Dollars

Like many other New England states, New Hampshire earns the most income from its finance, insurance, and real estate industries. Government is only the fifth-largest industry in terms of value of goods and services. What might help explain why government services in New Hampshire are not a larger part of the state economy?

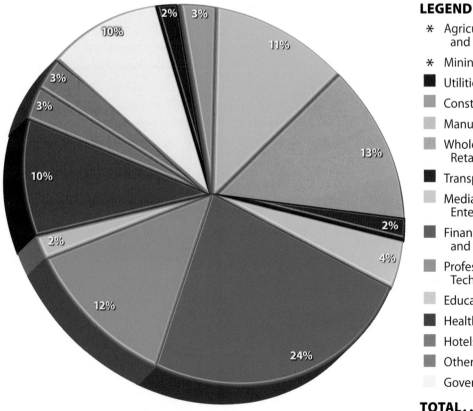

LEGEND

* Agriculture, Forestry, and Fishing	$215
* Mining	$19
■ Utilities	$1,191
Construction	$1,966
Manufacturing	$6,453
Wholesale and Retail Trade	$7,922
■ Transportation	$937
Media and Entertainment	$2,636
■ Finance, Insurance, and Real Estate	$14,501
Professional and Technical Services	$6,876
Education	$1,214
■ Health Care	$5,649
Hotels and Restaurants	$1,937
Other Services	$1,668
Government	$6,216
TOTAL	**$59,400**

*Less than 1%. Percentages may not add to 100 because of rounding.

Some farms collect sap from maple trees with plastic tubing. This method of collection requires less labor than using buckets, which must be emptied by hand.

Agriculture is another important industry in the state. There are more than 4,000 farms spread across New Hampshire, totaling more than 450,000 acres of land. The dairy industry generates more than $40 million each year. Fresh milk from the region is drunk locally or shipped to markets elsewhere in New England. Farmers across the country and beyond envy New Hampshire's dairy cows. These cows are sold as breeding animals around the world.

About 130 commercial dairy farms operate in New Hampshire.

I DIDN'T KNOW THAT!

New Hampshire does not have a state income tax or retail sales tax. There is also no tax on machinery and equipment. As a result, many manufacturing companies are located in the state.

Nursery and greenhouse products, dairy products, and apples are the state's major agricultural commodities. Hay, primarily used to feed livestock, is a valuable field crop, generating almost $5 million a year.

The Belknap Mill, in Laconia, once supported a bustling textile industry. Built in 1823, it is the oldest unchanged brick textile mill in the United States.

Dairy cattle are the main livestock raised in New Hampshire, but farmers also raise beef cattle, chickens, turkeys, and hogs.

Flounder, smelt, lobster, shrimp, and crab are all valuable products of New Hampshire's fishing industry.

Goods and Services

Manufactured goods are a crucial part of New Hampshire's economy. The state produces a variety of different types of industrial machinery, including computers and computer products, machinery for the pulp and paper industry, and bearings. Other important manufactured goods are paper products, rubber and plastic products, magazines and newspapers, and metals.

High-technology manufacturing remains an important industry in New Hampshire. There are companies devoted to producing circuit boards, optical fiber cables, and semiconductors. The state's high-technology workers are trained to make precision tools, including electricity-measuring devices, surgical tools, and optical lenses and instruments. Some 400 software producers also contribute to the state economy.

At DEKA Research and Development Corporation, located in an old Manchester mill, engineers work on innovative technology. Since 1982, the company has produced a robotic arm, a wheelchair that goes up stairs, and a simple water-purifying system.

While many residents produce things to sell, a large portion of the population works by performing services for others. Many of the state's service employees work in tourism. These people include servers and chefs in restaurants, amusement park employees, and hotel staff. Not all service workers cater to tourists. Government officials, teachers, doctors, accountants, and lawyers all work in the service industry.

Many people in New Hampshire like to stay well informed. It is easy to do given the high-quality print and online newspapers, radio stations, and television stations available throughout the state. The *New Hampshire Gazette* was the first newspaper in the state. It later evolved into the *Portsmouth Herald*. Among the state's daily newspapers, Manchester's *New Hampshire Union Leader*, Nashua's *Telegraph*, and the *Concord Monitor* are the best known.

New Hampshire's hotels and restaurants generate almost $2 billion a year.

I DIDN'T KNOW THAT!

The state's first free library was opened in 1833. In 1889 New Hampshire became the first state to enact a general library law, which supports local libraries throughout the state.

In the 1950s the USS *Albacore* was the fastest submarine ever designed. It was built at the Portsmouth Naval Shipyard.

The Seabrook nuclear power plant, located 13 miles south of Portsmouth, provides about 40 percent of the state's electricity. Some 45 percent of the electricity generated in New Hampshire comes from plants that burn natural gas or coal. About 7 percent is generated by **hydroelectric** plants.

The University of New Hampshire, in Durham, has about 12,000 undergraduates.

American Indians

Before European explorers arrived, approximately 12,000 American Indians lived in the New Hampshire area. Most of these people were Algonquian speakers, including people of the Abenaki and Pennacook groups. The number of American Indians in the region dropped dramatically in the 1600s due in part to fierce battles with the Mohawk to the west. Diseases that spread across the region also contributed to the decline of the American Indian population in the 1600s. Both the Abenaki and Pennacook lived by hunting, fishing, and farming. Many Abenaki and Pennacook hunting grounds spread into what are today western Maine and the lower Connecticut Valley.

Like other American Indian groups, the Pennacook and the Abenaki people fished through holes in the ice during winter.

The Abenaki made their homes, called wigwams, out of tree bark and animal skins. The Pennacook often built their villages around farms. In summer they moved to the coastal areas to fish. As the number of animals or fish in an area decreased, the American Indians moved on to areas with more plentiful food supplies.

Wigwams are huts or tents made by attaching skins or mats to a framework of poles.

I DIDN'T KNOW THAT!

The Abenaki belong to a collection of American Indian groups known as the *Wabanaki*, which means "People of the First Light."

The Abenaki group included the Ossipees and Pequawkets. The Pennacook group included the Amoskeags, Nashuas, Piscataquas, Souhegans, and Squamscots. The Sokokis and the Pocumtucks also lived in what is now New Hampshire.

Pennacook women often did their tasks as a group, socializing as they worked. Their responsibilities included preparing deer hides for clothing, working in the garden, maple sugaring, and making baskets.

The Mount Kearsarge Indian Museum, in Warner, is dedicated to educating visitors about American Indian groups as well as environmental conservation and nature. It hosts a music festival and powwow during the summer to highlight American Indian traditions, philosophy, and art.

Explorers

Viking sailors from Northern Europe may have visited the shores of what is now New Hampshire in the 11ᵗʰ century. Fishing ships from other parts of Europe may have explored the North American oceans as early as the 1400s. However, the first recorded exploration of the region was made by Englishman Martin Pring in 1603. He sailed up the Piscataqua River and is thought to have come ashore at what is now Portsmouth.

Pring was not alone in his interest in the area. In 1605 French explorer Samuel de Champlain arrived in the area and mapped the coastline. Then, in 1614, Captain John Smith of England sailed through the Isles of Shoals. He mapped the area for his country. England had a great interest in the area. In 1619, King James I established a Council for New England. He wanted to encourage people from England to settle in the region. Soon, small groups of settlers were sailing across the ocean to make a new life in New Hampshire.

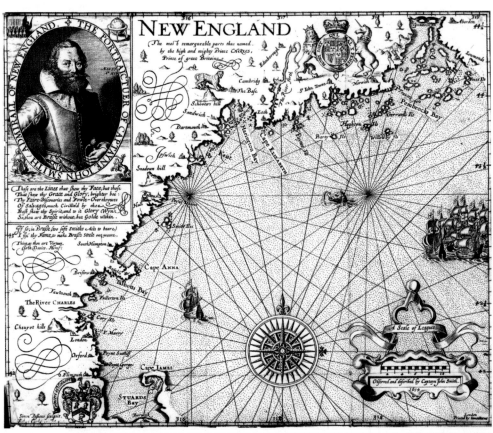

Captain John Smith drew a map of New England after his exploration in 1614. Smith was a well-known mapmaker and an author of exciting travelers' tales.

Timeline of Settlement

Early Exploration

1603 Martin Pring becomes the first European known to have explored the New Hampshire area.

1605 French explorer Samuel de Champlain maps the coast, including the Isles of Shoals.

1614 English captain John Smith visits the New England area, including what is now New Hampshire.

First Settlements

1622 English merchants John Mason and Sir Ferdinando Gorges are granted land in New England, which they divide into Maine and New Hampshire.

1623 Settlers are sent by John Mason to Odiorne's Point and then Dover to start the first permanent European settlements in what is now New Hampshire.

1638 Exeter and Hampton are established.

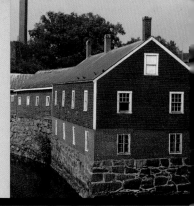

British Rule and American Revolution

1641 Massachusetts begins governing New Hampshire settlements.

1741 New Hampshire gets its own royal governor, separating from Massachusetts.

1774 The year before the battles of Lexington and Concord, rebels storm the British fort in Portsmouth.

1775 John Wentworth leaves office as the royal governor of New Hampshire colony. The American Revolution begins.

Independence and Statehood

1776 New Hampshire is the first colony to adopt its own constitution. Josiah Bartlett, who later serves as governor of New Hampshire, signs the Declaration of Independence.

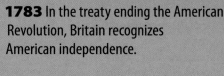

1783 In the treaty ending the American Revolution, Britain recognizes American independence.

1788 New Hampshire approves the new U.S. Constitution and becomes the ninth state in the Union.

Early Settlers

The English government issued many overlapping and confusing land grants in the New Hampshire region. In 1622, Captain John Mason and Sir Ferdinando Gorges were both given grants for the land between the Kennebec and Merrimack Rivers. The two men split the land between them, dividing it at the Piscataqua River. Gorges' region east of the river became the province of Maine. Mason named his region New Hampshire.

Map of Settlements and Resources in Early New Hampshire

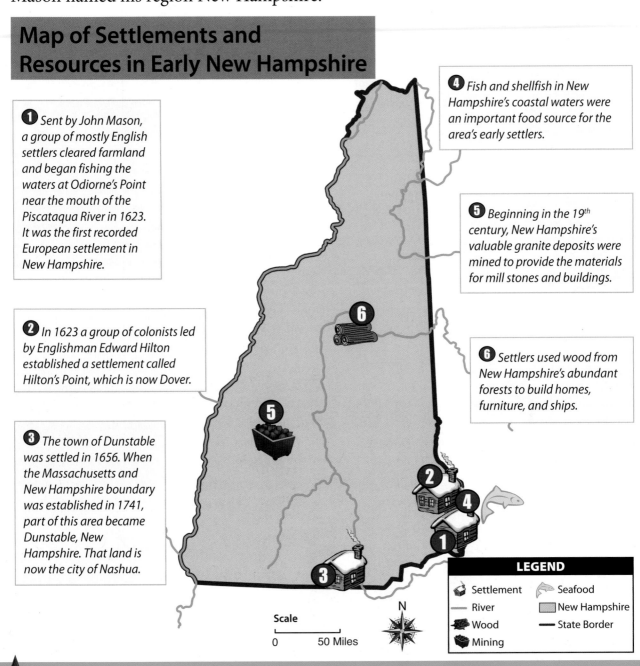

1 Sent by John Mason, a group of mostly English settlers cleared farmland and began fishing the waters at Odiorne's Point near the mouth of the Piscataqua River in 1623. It was the first recorded European settlement in New Hampshire.

2 In 1623 a group of colonists led by Englishman Edward Hilton established a settlement called Hilton's Point, which is now Dover.

3 The town of Dunstable was settled in 1656. When the Massachusetts and New Hampshire boundary was established in 1741, part of this area became Dunstable, New Hampshire. That land is now the city of Nashua.

4 Fish and shellfish in New Hampshire's coastal waters were an important food source for the area's early settlers.

5 Beginning in the 19th century, New Hampshire's valuable granite deposits were mined to provide the materials for mill stones and buildings.

6 Settlers used wood from New Hampshire's abundant forests to build homes, furniture, and ships.

LEGEND

Settlement | Seafood
River | New Hampshire
Wood | State Border
Mining

Scale
0   50 Miles

N

Scotsman David Thomson and a group of settlers were given permission to colonize a smaller piece of land in the New Hampshire area. In 1623 they created a settlement called Odiorne's Point.

In 1638 the towns of Exeter and Hampton were established. Dover, Portsmouth, Hampton, and Exeter were the only permanent settlements in the area for several decades. During the middle and late 1600s, New Hampshire was often governed by Massachusetts, and the two colonies shared the same royal governor until 1741. In that year New Hampshire became independent of Massachusetts and was given its own royal governor.

By the 1760s British rule had worn thin with the colonists. When the American Revolution began in 1775, soldiers from New Hampshire took up arms against Britain and battled for eight years for independence. New Hampshire's trade and economy soared after independence, and more people rushed to the state to find work and start a new life.

Europeans settled Odiorne's Point, now part of Rye, near what is today Portsmouth.

Captain Martin Pring did not venture far into New Hampshire in 1603. He explored the coastline and only a short distance into the interior.

After establishing a settlement in Jamestown, Virginia, in 1607, Captain John Smith spent many years surveying unexplored parts of New England. His book, *A Description of New England*, led the Pilgrims to Massachusetts.

John Mason served as vice admiral for New England in 1635 but died before ever reaching New Hampshire. Mason named the state after the British town of Hampshire, where he had lived as a young man.

Notable People

Many notable people from New Hampshire have contributed to the development of their state and their country. They have served on the battlefields of many wars, in the White House, and on the Supreme Court. Residents of the Granite State have also been activists and educators, authors and journalists, and inventors and astronauts.

JOHN STARK
(1728–1822)

General John Stark, born in Londonderry in 1728, commanded troops during the American Revolution. Stark's regiment helped defend Bunker Hill, and Stark led troops, with John Sullivan, in the battles of Trenton in 1776 and Princeton in 1777. It was General Stark who encouraged his soldiers to "Live Free or Die," which became the state motto in 1945. When he died in 1822, at the age of 93, this brave military leader was one of the last surviving Continental Army generals.

FRANKLIN PIERCE
(1804–1869)

Born in Hillsboro in 1804, Franklin Pierce served as the 14th president of the United States from 1853 to 1857. The first and only New Hampshire citizen to become president, Pierce was a congressman, senator, lawyer, and Mexican-American War general. As president, he promoted American expansion and trade with other countries. As a father, he suffered great personal loss, mourning the death of his three children.

MARY BAKER EDDY
(1821–1910)

Born near Concord in 1821, Mary Baker Eddy founded the Christian Science religion after decades of poor health. She explained her understanding of healing through prayer in *Science and Health*, published in 1875. In 1908, Mary Baker Eddy founded the *Christian Science Monitor*, an award-winning newspaper.

ALAN B. SHEPARD JR.
(1923–1998)

Shepard, from East Derry, served in World War II after graduating from the U.S. Naval Academy. In 1961, he became the first American to travel into space. As captain of *Apollo 14*, he later became one of the first people to walk on the Moon. Alan B. Shepard Jr. proved himself a pioneer of manned space flight.

DAVID SOUTER
(1939–)

David Souter served as an associate justice of the U.S. Supreme Court from 1990 to 2009. Born in Massachusetts in 1939, he moved to Weare as a child and returned to live in Concord after earning a law degree at Harvard University. Souter, considered a conservative judge when George H. W. Bush appointed him, ended his time on the bench known as a liberal.

I DIDN'T KNOW THAT!

S. Christa McAuliffe (1948–1986) from Concord was chosen by the National Aeronautics and Space Administration to be the first teacher, and private citizen, in space. She and six others were killed in the explosion of the space shuttle *Challenger* in 1986.

Ken Burns (1953–) is a documentary filmmaker who lives in Walpole. His best-known productions are *The Civil War*, *Baseball*, *Jazz*, and *The National Parks: America's Best Ideas*.

Population

I n the mid-1800s many of the people in New Hampshire were of British **ancestry**. As the state became more industrialized, people moved there to work in the factories and mills. Since that time the population has continued to grow. By the end of 2010 more than 1.3 million Americans lived in the state.

People who live in New Hampshire tend to be well educated. More than 87 percent of residents 25 years of age or older have graduated from high school. Nearly 29 percent of people in that age group are college graduates. Both figures are above the national average.

New Hampshire Population 1950–2010

Of all the states, New Hampshire ranks 42nd in population. Its population has almost doubled since 1970, however. What factors might explain the fast rate of growth since 1970?

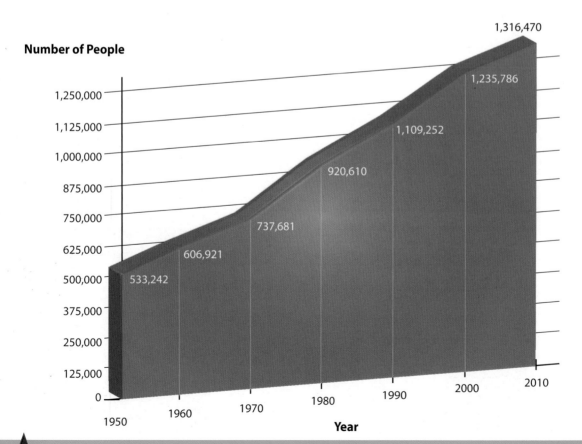

Number of People

- 1,316,470
- 1,235,786
- 1,109,252
- 920,610
- 737,681
- 606,921
- 533,242

1,250,000
1,125,000
1,000,000
875,000
750,000
625,000
500,000
375,000
250,000
125,000
0

1950 1960 1970 1980 1990 2000 2010

Year

Almost 22 percent of New Hampshire's population is below the age of 18.

Most people in New Hampshire are of European descent, 2 percent of the population is Asian American, and 1.4 percent is African American.

The population density of New Hampshire is about 147 people per square mile of land. The average for the nation is 87 people per square mile.

The most-populated cities in New Hampshire are Manchester, Nashua, and Concord.

Many people in New Hampshire live in small towns and rural areas.

Politics and Government

New Hampshire's government is made up of three branches. They arc the executive, legislative, and judicial. The governor and the executive council belong to the executive branch. The governor cannot spend money without the council's approval. The executive branch ensures that laws are carried out.

The legislature of New Hampshire is called the General Court. It is made up of the state Senate, which has 24 members, and the state House of Representatives, with 400 members. The House of Representatives has more members than any chamber of any other state legislature in the country.

The New Hampshire State House in Concord, completed in 1819, is made of local granite. On its front lawn stands a statue of the only U.S. president from New Hampshire, Franklin Pierce.

In 1944, representatives from 44 countries came to Bretton Woods to plan for an international monetary system. The World Bank and the International Monetary Fund were created at this historic meeting in New Hampshire.

The legislature writes new laws and changes or updates old ones. Both the Senate and the House of Representatives need to agree on a bill before it is forwarded to the governor for approval.

The third branch, the judicial, is made up of the courts. The highest court is the Supreme Court, which consists of a chief justice and four associate judges. There are lower district and municipal courts in this branch as well. The judicial branch is in charge of enforcing and interpreting state laws.

The state song of New Hampshire is called "Old New Hampshire."

Here is an excerpt from the song:

*With a skill that knows
    no measure,
From the golden store of Fate
God, in His great love
    and wisdom,
Made the rugged
    Granite State;
Made the lakes, the fields,
    the forests;
Made the Rivers and the rills;
Made the bubbling, crystal
    fountains
Of New Hampshire's
    Granite Hills*

Chorus:
*Old New Hampshire,
    Old New Hampshire
Old New Hampshire
    Grand and Great
We will sing of Old
    New Hampshire,
Of he dear old Granite State*

Cultural Groups

New Hampshire developed into an industrial center in the early 1900s, and people from all over the world moved to the state. Immigrants, especially those from Scotland, England, The Netherlands, France, Poland, Greece, Ireland, and Canada, provided rapidly growing industries with an inexpensive workforce. This steady flow of immigrants to New Hampshire, which lasted until the 1920s, also created a **diverse** and exciting culture in the state.

Recent immigrants to New Hampshire include Bosnian Muslims. They maintain their traditions and contribute to the state's cultural diversity.

Traditional Morris dancing, still practiced in England as well as New Hampshire, is thought to be a celebration of spring.

As more immigrants arrived in an area, they began forming ethnic neighborhoods. In this new country, newcomers could find a community that spoke their native language, ate familiar foods, and understood their customs and traditions. Some ethnic areas grew quickly and worked hard to preserve their heritage. They continue to do so today.

Some people in New Hampshire celebrate their culture through food. Today, ethnic restaurants offer delicious dishes from countries such as China, Italy, Poland, and Greece. Other groups celebrate their culture through music and dancing. Morris dancing is an old English form of dancing that is practiced in southwestern New Hampshire. This lively dance is performed for an audience. The dancers, accompanied by a live musician, wear bells on their legs and wave sticks and handkerchiefs. Teams of Morris dancers often tour New England, with each team having its own special "kit," or uniform.

I DIDN'T KNOW THAT!

Sarah Josepha Hale, born in Newport in 1788, wrote the poem *Mary Had a Little Lamb*. She also campaigned to establish Thanksgiving as a holiday for all Americans in 1863.

Some New Hampshire mill owners recruited workers straight from the immigration center on Ellis Island in New York.

The official state language is English, but many other languages are spoken in New Hampshire. A large number of citizens speak Spanish, French, Greek, or German with their families at home.

Arts Jubilee is an annual summer concert series held in North Conway Village. Musical acts range from Celtic to classical. Other events include the Great Water Music Festival at Lake Winnipesaukee and the New Hampshire Music Festival.

Arts and Entertainment

New Hampshire has been home to many successful writers. Among them is novelist John Irving. Born in Exeter, Irving wrote his first novel in 1969. He achieved widespread renown when his popular fourth novel, *The World According to Garp*, was published in 1978. *The Hotel New Hampshire, The Cider House Rules, A Prayer for Owen Meany*, and *A Widow for One Year* have all brought further success to this talented author. They have also brought recognition to his home state, in which many of his novels are set.

Music and dance are also popular arts in the state. Ballet New England, in Portsmouth, stages ballet performances throughout the year. Several orchestras, including the Monadnock Chorus and Orchestra and the New Hampshire Philharmonic Orchestra in Manchester, appeal to classical music lovers. The superior acoustics of Music Hall, in Portsmouth, guarantees an unbeatable performance by the many talented musicians, actors, and dancers who grace its stage. Music Hall brings exciting touring productions to New Hampshire.

Several of John Irving's novels have been made into successful movies. Irving won an Academy Award for the The Cider House Rules *screenplay in 2000.*

In 1885 the famous sculptor Augustus Saint-Gaudens set up a house and studio in Cornish. Today a gilded bronze cast of his Amor Caritas overlooks the courtyard.

Audiences crowd theaters throughout the state to experience excellent live drama. The Seacoast Repertory Theater is one of the top regional theaters in the area. The Celebrity Series in Durham presents world-class dance, music, and theater.

The numerous art galleries and museums in New Hampshire feature local and international works of art. The best in the state include the Hood Museum of Art at Dartmouth College in Hanover and the Currier Gallery of Art in Manchester. In Cornish the studio of Irish-born sculptor Augustus Saint-Gaudens is now a historic site that features the artist's works as well as exhibits of new artists.

I DIDN'T KNOW THAT!

J. D. Salinger, a Cornish resident, wrote the legendary yet controversial novel *Catcher in the Rye*. He died in 2010 at the age of 91.

The Cornish Hill Pottery Company decorates pots with the same technique used by early North American and European potters. The technique is called "slip trailing." A creamy clay and water mixture, called the slip, is put on nearly hardened pots, which adds a natural color to the pieces.

In Holderness, film buffs can take a sailing tour to view the sights featured in the Oscar-winning 1981 film *On Golden Pond*. Squam Lake was the setting for many scenes in the classic movie.

Actress and singer Mandy Moore was born in Nashua in 1984. She has appeared in several films, including *The Princess Diaries* and *Chasing Liberty*.

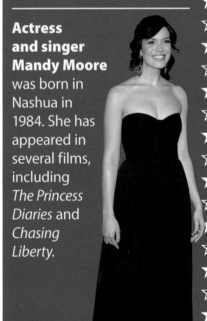

Sports

New Hampshire's residents are kept busy with the state's many outdoor facilities and recreation areas. Cycling is a popular way to see the area and get some exercise. Mountain bikers can explore the trails through the White Mountains and through parks such as Franconia Notch State Park. The more daring adventurer can try rock climbing. For those who prefer to have their feet on the ground, hiking is an exciting sport in New Hampshire. Trails wind up to the top of the White Mountain peaks, offering hikers sensational views and a glimpse of the area's wildlife.

More than 2 million skiers and snowboarders travel to New Hampshire each year to test their skills on the slopes. Attitash Bear Peak is the largest ski resort in the state. Skiers also visit Black Mountain, Cannon Mountain, Cranmore, and Mount Sunapee for a challenge. For those who prefer flatter terrain, Jackson offers some of the best cross-country skiing in the eastern United States.

New Hampshire offers challenging climbing for adventurers of all levels.

New Hampshire does not have teams in the major professional sports leagues, but that does not mean there is a shortage of sports. The men and women who play for the University of New Hampshire Wildcats fill arenas with cheering fans when they take to the fields, skate onto the ice in hockey, or suit up for basketball or volleyball. Many Wildcats players have been awarded national prizes and have enjoyed professional careers in their sports.

One of the greatest American downhill skiers is New Hampshire's Bode Miller. He is a two-time World Cup overall champion and five-time Olympic medalist. At the 2010 Winter Olympics, Miller won a gold medal in the super combined event.

Bode Miller has won more Olympic medals than any other American downhill skier. He learned to ski and snowboard as a child at Cannon Mountain.

I DIDN'T KNOW THAT!

Spring and summer fishing are popular in the hundreds of lakes and streams in the state.

Chris Carpenter, born in Exeter, pitches for the St. Louis Cardinals. He was drafted in the first round of the 1993 amateur draft.

Hilary Knight, born in 1989 in Hanover, played on the U.S. women's hockey team at the 2010 Winter Olympics. The Americans won the silver medal in women's hockey.

National Averages Comparison

T he United States is a federal republic, consisting of fifty states and the District of Columbia. Alaska and Hawai'i are the only non-contiguous, or non-touching, states in the nation. Today, the United States of America is the third-largest country in the world in population. The United States Census Bureau takes a census, or count of all the people, every ten years. It also regularly collects other kinds of data about the population and the economy. How does New Hampshire compare with the national average?

Comparison Chart

United States 2010 Census Data *	USA	New Hampshire
Admission to Union	NA	June 21, 1788
Land Area (in square miles)	3,537,438.44	8,968.10
Population Total	308,745,538	1,316,470
Population Density (people per square mile)	87.28	146.79
Population Percentage Change (April 1, 2000, to April 1, 2010)	9.7%	6.5%
White Persons (percent)	72.4%	93.9%
Black Persons (percent)	12.6%	1.1%
American Indian and Alaska Native Persons (percent)	0.9%	0.2%
Asian Persons (percent)	4.8%	2.2%
Native Hawaiian and Other Pacific Islander Persons (percent)	0.2%	—
Some Other Race (percent)	6.2%	0.9%
Persons Reporting Two or More Races (percent)	2.9%	1.6%
Persons of Hispanic or Latino Origin (percent)	16.3%	2.8%
Not of Hispanic or Latino Origin (percent)	83.7%	97.2%
Median Household Income	$52,029	$63,235
Percentage of People Age 25 or Over Who Have Graduated from High School	80.4%	87.4%

*All figures are based on the 2010 United States Census, with the exception of the last two items. Percentages may not add to 100 because of rounding.

How to Improve My Community

S trong communities make strong states. Think about what features are important in your community. What do you value? Education? Health? Forests? Safety? Beautiful spaces? Government works to help citizens create ideal living conditions that are fair to all by providing services in communities. Consider what changes you could make in your community. How would they improve your state as a whole? Using this concept web as a guide, write a report that outlines the features you think are most important in your community and what improvements could be made. A strong state needs strong communities.

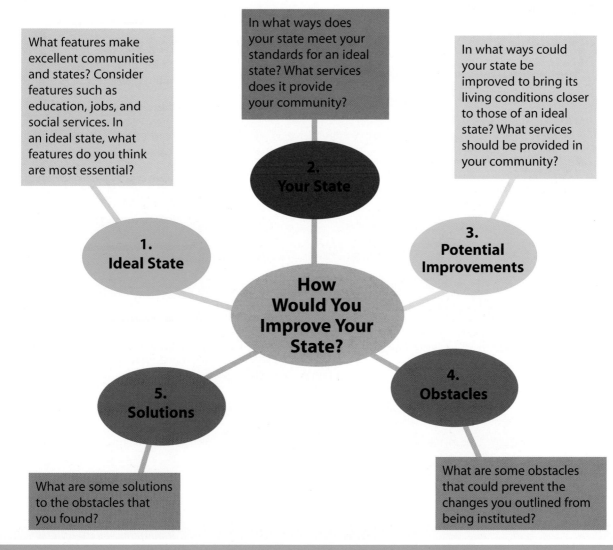

What features make excellent communities and states? Consider features such as education, jobs, and social services. In an ideal state, what features do you think are most essential?

In what ways does your state meet your standards for an ideal state? What services does it provide your community?

In what ways could your state be improved to bring its living conditions closer to those of an ideal state? What services should be provided in your community?

**2.
Your State**

**1.
Ideal State**

**3.
Potential
Improvements**

**How
Would You
Improve Your
State?**

**5.
Solutions**

**4.
Obstacles**

What are some solutions to the obstacles that you found?

What are some obstacles that could prevent the changes you outlined from being instituted?

Exercise Your Mind!

Think about these questions and then use your research skills to find the answers and learn more fascinating facts about New Hampshire. A teacher, librarian, or parent may be able to help you locate the best sources to use in your research.

1 How did skiing come to New Hampshire?

2 Where was the first potato planted in the United States?

3 What is the Great Bay Estuary?

4 What did New Hampshire have to do with the Russo-Japanese War?

5 Where is the longest covered bridge in the United States?

6 Peterborough was the inspiration for what Pulitzer Prize-winning play?

7 What did Earl Tupper of New Hampshire invent?

8 What did a Concord man invent in 1787?

Words to Know

ancestry: the people from whom an individual or group is descended

beryl: a precious stone that is usually green

caboose: the last car on a freight train

constitution: the laws and principles under which a government runs a state or country

Continental Army: the name of the U.S. Army during the American Revolution

diverse: made up of different kinds

endangered: at risk of becoming extinct

glaciers: large bodies of ice that move very slowly

hydroelectric: using waterpower to create electricity

presidential primary election: an election to choose a political party's presidential candidate

quarries: open pits from which stone is mined

railroad ties: wooden beams laid between railroad tracks to support the rails

revolutionary: a person or group committed to political or social change

Index

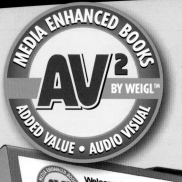

Log on to www.av2books.com

AV² by Weigl brings you media enhanced books that support active learning. Go to www.av2books.com, and enter the special code found on page 2 of this book. You will gain access to enriched and enhanced content that supplements and complements this book. Content includes video, audio, web links, quizzes, a slide show, and activities.

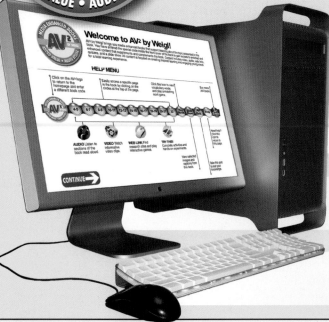

Audio
Listen to sections of the book read aloud.

Video
Watch informative video clips.

Embedded Weblinks
Gain additional information for research.

Try This!
Complete activities and hands-on experiments.

WHAT'S ONLINE?

Try This!	Embedded Weblinks	Video	EXTRA FEATURES
Test your knowledge of the state in a mapping activity.	Discover more attractions in New Hampshire.	Watch a video introduction to New Hampshire.	
Find out more about precipitation in your city.	Learn more about the history of the state.	Watch a video about the features of the state.	**Audio** Listen to sections of the book read aloud.
Plan what attractions you would like to visit in the state.	Learn the full lyrics of the state song.		**Key Words** Study vocabulary, and complete a matching word activity.
Learn more about the early natural resources of the state.			
Write a biography about a notable resident of New Hampshire.			**Slide Show** View images and captions, and prepare a presentation.
Complete an educational census activity.			**Quizzes** Test your knowledge.

AV² was built to bridge the gap between print and digital. We encourage you to tell us what you like and what you want to see in the future.

Sign up to be an AV² Ambassador at www.av2books.com/ambassador.

Due to the dynamic nature of the Internet, some of the URLs and activities provided as part of AV² by Weigl may have changed or ceased to exist. AV² by Weigl accepts no responsibility for any such changes. All media enhanced books are regularly monitored to update addresses and sites in a timely manner. Contact AV² by Weigl at 1-866-649-3445 or av2books@weigl.com with any questions, comments, or feedback.